Racing Dreams
A SPORT CAR COLORING BOOK

THIS BOOK BELONGS TO

Index

01 Bmw M3 GTS
02 Lamborghini Aventador
03 Lamborghini Countatch
04 Ferrari F40
05 Audi R8 GT3
06 Porsche 918
07 Porsche 911 2.7
08 Nissan GTR R35
09 Volkswagen Golf GTI
10 Ac Cobra
11 Ferrari LaFerrari
12 Pagani Zonda R
13 Ferrari 250 GTO
14 McLaren F1 GTR
15 Bmw M3 E36

16 Lexus LFA
17 Mercedes-Benz SLS GT3
18 Ferrari 488 Pista
19 Chevrolet Corvette ZR1
20 McLaren 675LT
21 Mazda 787B
22 Nissan 350Z
23 Audi RS4 V8 Avant
24 Porsche 911 GT3 RS
25 Lamborghini Huracan
26 Alfa Romeo 4C
27 Datsun 280Z
28 Porsche 356
29 Renault Clio RS
30 Honda S2000

RACING DREAMS

*Revving Up the Fun:
Discovering the Excitement of Sport Cars*

Experience the speed and power of some of history's most impressive machines with this exciting coloring book. From classic cars from yesterday to today's futuristic hypercars, you're sure to be immersed in a world full of vibrant illustrations. Learn about these powerful vehicles while discovering their captivating past - without even leaving your seat.

01 BMW M3 GTS

The BMW M3 GTS is a track-ready monster, boasting an awe-inspiring 4.4 liter V8 engine that produces 450 horsepower and 325 lb-ft of torque with its 7 speed dual clutch transmission. Its lightweight design includes a carbon fiber roof, hood and front splitter; in addition to the sport tuned suspension for advanced aerodynamics which allows it to hit 190 mph top speed from 0 - 60mph under just 4.4 seconds.

02 Lamborghini Aventador

The Lamborghini Aventador is a thrill seeker's dream. Since its debut in 2011, this powerful V12 engine sports car has continued to be produced with immense power and speed - 740 horsepower, 509 lb-ft of torque, 0-60 mph acceleration rate in an astonishing 2.9 seconds and top speed of 217 mph! The design of the Aventador shows off sharp angles and aggressive lines that come alive in vibrant colors ranging from stealthy black to bright yellow. Not surprisingly, driving enthusiasts everywhere appreciate its extraordinary performance as much as they admire its eye catching style.

03 Lamborghini Countatch

The Lamborghini Countach is an iconic, mid-engine sports car that was created by the Italian automotive company between 1974 and 1990. Marcello Gandini designed this revolutionary vehicle - it featured a stylish wedge shape with defining sharp lines, scissor doors, and prominent air intakes. As one of the most recognizable cars in history, the Countach will always be remembered as a legendary symbol of power and confidence on the roads.

04 FERRARI F40

To commemorate Ferrari's 40th anniversary, the renowned Italian automaker produced the remarkable F40 from 1987 to 1992. This high-performance sports car is equipped with a mid-engine and rear-wheel drive system for superior handling capabilities. Its 2.9L V8 engine boasts an impressive 478 horsepower and 425 lb-ft of torque, allowing it to reach an incredible top speed of 201 mph while accelerating from 0 - 60 mph in a mere 3.8 seconds! The F40 is truly iconic, combining power and precision like no other vehicle before it. The F40 is crafted with an exquisite combination of lightweight materials such as carbon fiber and Kevlar, designed to be both aerodynamic and attractive.

05   AUDI R8 GT3

The Audi R8 GT3 is a truly remarkable feat of automotive engineering. This competition-ready racing car, based on the classic R8 supercar and boasting an incredible 5.2L V10 engine with up to 585 horsepower at its disposal, can accelerate from 0 to 186 mph in no time thanks to its 6-speed sequential gearbox. Every detail has been carefully considered while crafting this beastly machine, aerodynamics and weight distribution optimized via intricate suspension systems coupled with lightweight carbon fiber construction make it unbeatable when it comes down beating other cars around track curves.

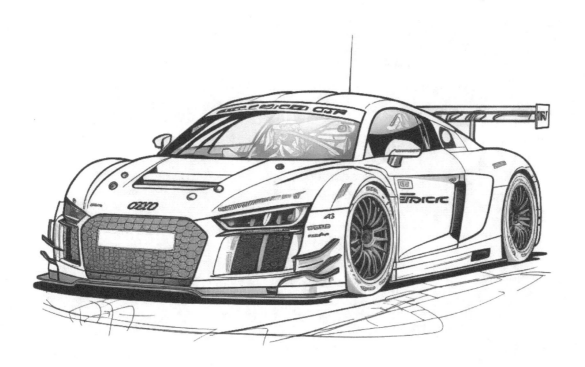

06 PORSCHE 918

The Porsche 918 is a revolutionary hybrid supercar that stands in its own class of performance vehicles. Featuring an incredibly powerful 4.6-liter V8 engine combined with electric motors, this car boasts 887 horsepower and 944 lb-ft of torque — meaning the 0 to 60 time isn't even close: 2.2 seconds! Plus, it can reach top speeds as high as 214 mph thanks to its lightweight carbon fiber body structure for improved aerodynamics plus advanced suspension and braking systems crafted just by Porsche engineers themselves; making the remarkable 918 one of the most coveted luxury cars ever created by this timeless German brand which lives on today through sheer mechanical excellence.

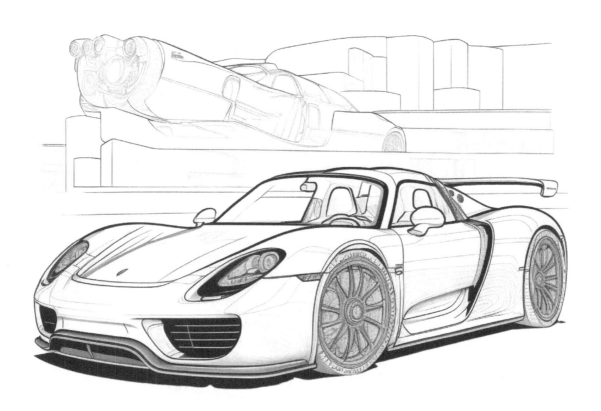

07 PORSCHE 911 2.7

The Porsche 911 2.7 is a classic sports car that has captivated and enthralled enthusiasts for generations thanks to its iconic design, incredible performance potential, and remarkable handling capabilities. Featuring the unmistakable sleek look of classic Porsches past combined with an impressive 150 horsepower flat-six engine capable of accelerating from 0 to 60 mph in 6 seconds and reaching speeds up to 130 miles per hour, this legendary ride deserves every accolade it receives as one of the most accomplished cars ever produced by Porsche.

08 NISSAN GTR R35

The Nissan GTR R35 is a truly magnificent machine, combining beauty and power in one sleek package. With its remarkable 3.8-liter V6 engine pumping out 600 horsepower and 481 lb-ft of torque, the car can reach speeds up to 196 mph while going from 0 to 60 mph in just 2.7 seconds. It's equipped with an advanced all-wheel drive system for exceptional road control as well as technology inspired suspension that adjusts for optimal performance on any terrain - making it perfect for any daring driver looking to conquer their wildest dreams behind the wheel of this unforgettable supercar.

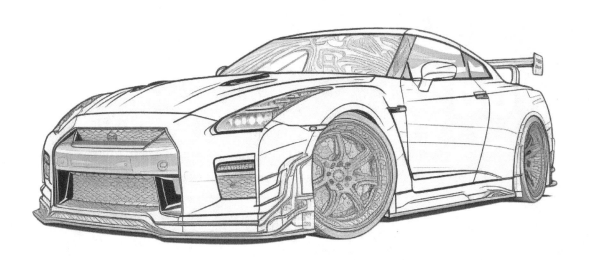

09 Volkswagen Golf GTI

The Volkswagen Golf GTI 1977 — the first of its kind — revolutionized automotive design. Its 1.6-liter four-cylinder engine was capable of a powerful 110 horsepower and 110 lb-ft torque that had drivers reaching speeds up to an impressive 110 mph, while going from 0 to 60 in just 9 seconds. In addition, it featured sporty suspensions, front/rear spoilers and unique interior designs with special seats - all presented within a stylish three door hatchback body style equipped with five manual transmission gears for ultimate control on the road.

10 AC Cobra

The cult classic AC Cobra, also known as the Shelby Cobra, dominated its racing era with astonishing speed and power. Developed by American car designer Carroll Shelby in collaboration with British manufacturer AC Cars, this iconic sports car contained a powerful Ford V8 engine under its lightweight fiberglass body - enabling it to reach speeds of up to 150 mph from 0-60mph in only 4 seconds. This masterful feat made the beloved Cobras sought after among race fans for both their roadster and coupe versions over five years between 1962-1967.

11 Ferrari LaFerrari

Ferrari has always been synonymous with performance and the LaFerrari, their pinnacle limited-edition hybrid supercar, is no exception. With its cutting edge technology like active suspension and dual clutch transmission paired with a V12 engine augmented by electric motors to reach an astonishing 949 horsepower output — this car can go from 0 to 60 mph in only 3 seconds on its way up 217mph! Thanks to just 500 units produced worldwide between 2013 and 2016, owning one of these breathtaking machines makes you truly part of Ferrari's elite club.

12 Pagani Zonda R

Pagani's legendary Zonda R is the epitome of a supercar. Built to conquer any track, this limited-edition racer features an awe-inspiring 6.0L V12 engine that yields 750 horsepower and 524 lb-ft of torque, allowing it to reach 217 mph with a 0—60 time in just 2.5 seconds! Constructed from lightweight carbon fiber and titanium for superior agility on the circuit coupled with advanced aerodynamics and its own proprietary sequential gearbox; only 15 examples were ever produced making them extremely exclusive - coveted by collectors across the globe.

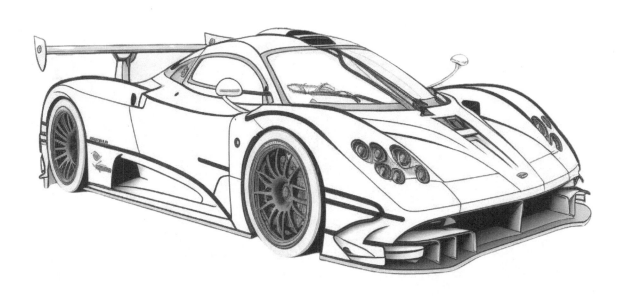

13 Ferrari 250 GTO

The Ferrari 250 GTO is a coveted classic, earning its place in the world's most sought-after and valuable cars. Produced between 1962 and 1964 with only 36 units made, this beauty was designed to perform on the track, a 3.0 liter V12 engine producing 300 horsepower reaches speeds of 174 mph while accelerating from 0 - 60 mph in just 6.1 seconds! With sleek aerodynamics, superior handling capabilities and an iconic design that has stood the test of time--the Ferrari 250 GTO is truly one for motorsport aficionados everywhere.

14 McLaren F1 GTR

The McLaren F1 GTR: a race car like no other. With its 6.1-liter V12 engine producing an impressive 600 horsepower and reaching 0 to 60 mph in only 3.2 seconds, this beast of machine boasts a top speed of 225 mph - all thanks to advanced aerodynamics such as the large rear wing and diffuser that maximize performance on the track.

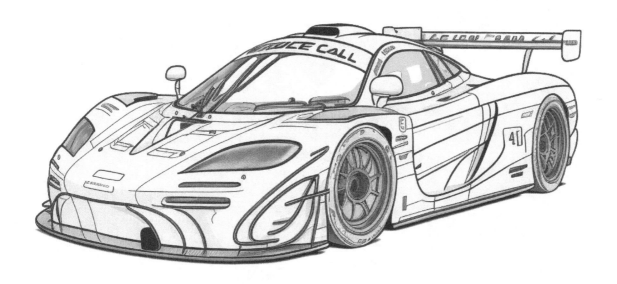

15 BMW M3 E36

The BMW M3 E36 3.2 is a timeless sports car that still thrills today — and it's no wonder why! Boasting an incomparable 321 horses, 236 lb-ft of torque, and top speed of 155 mph under the hood along with enhanced suspension for improved handling/performance; this classic beauty can rocket from 0 to 60 mph in only 5.5 seconds thanks to its six-speed manual transmission & rear wheel drive - making it one seriously fast yet stylish ride produced by BMW Europe between 1992—1999 delighting all enthusiasts alike

16　Lexus LFA

The Lexus LFA is a rare, high-performance sports car mastered for adrenaline seekers. Its 4.8-liter V10 engine churns out 552 horsepower and 354 lb-ft of torque that zooms from 0 to 60 mph in just 3.6 seconds while reaching an extraordinary top speed of 202 mph - all due to its sleek aerodynamic body complemented by lightweight materials ensuring maximum agility behind the wheel! With only 500 units made worldwide, it's no surprise this collector's item has become sought after among those dreaming about intensely thrilling driving experiences.

17 Mercedes-Benz SLS GT3

The Mercedes-Benz SLS GT3 is a powerhouse of performance, crafted for the thrill of track racing. Packing in an impressive 6.3L V8 engine and reaching speeds up to 190mph, this agile vehicle features adjustable suspension plus dual hydraulic calipers to ensure dependable braking power when you need it most. With four-point harnesses affixed on the racing seats and an LCD display delivering driver details at your fingertips, you will have all the comfort needed to navigate those thrilling curves in that circuit. And turning heads both inside and out; The Mercedes Benz SLS is a pure embodiment of endurance motorsport excitement, from its aerodynamic body panels to the striking GT3 livery exterior fixtures including an iconic rear wing.

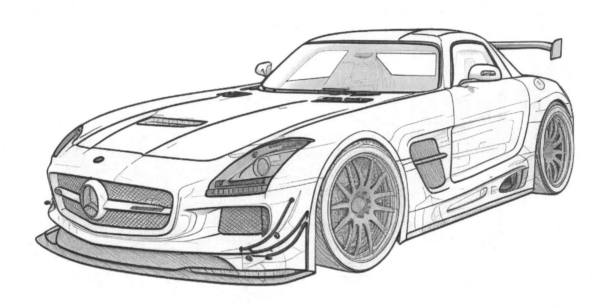

18 Ferrari 488 Pista

The 488 Pista from Ferrari is an absolute beast ! Equipped with a 3.9L V8 twin-turbo engine, this vehicle can deliver up to 710 horsepower and 760 Nm of torque that lets it reach 0-60 mph in under three seconds flat - reaching 211mph at its peak speed. Additionally, the Brembo carbon ceramic brakes guarantee smooth stopping power while the magnetorheological suspension combines perfectly with Ferraris Side Slip Control system for optimal handling performance on any track or road surface imaginable — all produced without sacrificing style as evidenced by its iconic black & red body adorned with aerodynamic elements including wheels designed specifically to reduce drag during high speeds runs.

19 Chevrolet Corvette ZR1

Experience the ultimate in performance with a sleek, eye-catching design - that is what you get from the Chevrolet Corvette ZR1 C6. Its 6.2L Supercharged V8 engine delivers power like no other vehicle on the market — cranking out an awe-inspiring 638 horsepower and 819 lb ft of torque for maximum thrills! Drivers have complete control at their fingertips thanks to its close ratio six speed manual transmission, along with powerful brakes featuring cross drilled rotors and advanced traction control system catered towards superior handling & safety measures. Sit behind 19"x10" front wheels wrapped around Michelin Pilot Sport 2 tires while 20" x 12" rear wheels offer fierce agility & style when taking corners at break neck speeds on your next ride in this two seated modern marvel.

20 McLaren 675LT

The McLaren 675LT is the ultimate expression of boundary-pushing performance and stylish design. Boasting a more aggressive body kit, improved aerodynamics, an adjustable suspension system and lightweight carbon fiber build - not to mention its twin turbocharged V8 engine's awe-inspiring power output of 675hp that rockets it from 0-60 in a mere 2.9 seconds. Any driver lucky enough to take command of this vehicle will stand out wherever they go with these extraordinary capabilities at their fingertips.

21   MAZDA 787B

The Mazda 787B revolutionized the racing industry with its awe-inspiring 4-rotor Wankel rotary engine that unleashed an incredible 700 horsepower. With a lightweight carbon fiber body, the 787B had superb acceleration and could reach mindboggling speeds of over 240 mph. Its aerodynamic design lent it superior speed in races like 24 Hours of Le Mans where it made history as the first Japanese car to ever win both 1st place overall and Group C category in 1991 - forever establishing itself as one of most iconic race cars to date.

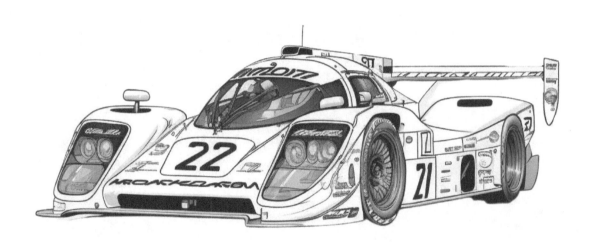

22 Nissan 350Z

With its powerful 306-horsepower 3.5L V6 engine, the Nissan 350Z is a dream come true for sports car aficionados! This two-door coupe accelerates from 0 to 60 mph in just 5.5 seconds and has an impressive top speed of 156 mph — all thanks to its aerodynamically designed body and sharp handling capabilities. The advanced technology used in this vehicle brings it up to date with modern amenities while still providing classic performance that can't be matched by any other make or model.

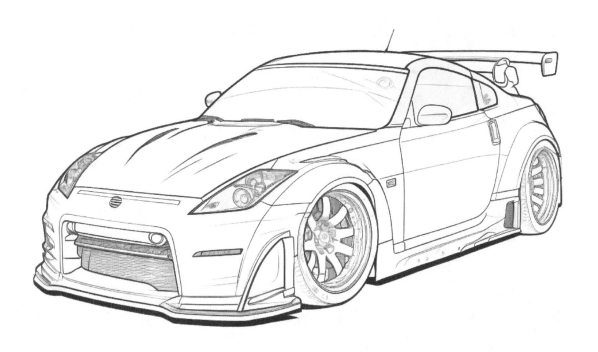

23 Audi RS4 V8 Avant

Accelerating from 0 to 60mph in a remarkable 4.7 seconds, the Audi RS4 V8 Avant is an exceptional combination of high-performance, luxury and style. Boasting a powerful 4.2 liter V8 engine which generates 420 horsepower with 317 lb-ft torque; advanced suspension and braking systems for optimal handling stability; all wheel drive technology for improved traction on uneven terrain surfaces - this station wagon leaves nothing wanting!

24 Porsche 911 GT3 RS

The Porsche 911 GT3 RS (991.2) is an engineering marvel that blends head-turning aesthetic with industry-leading technology. Powered by a 4.0 liter flat-six engine, this track ready machine pushes 500 horsepower and 339 lb ft of torque through its seven speed PDK transmission to send it hurtling from 0 - 60 mph in just 3 exhilarating seconds; topping out at 193mph! Lightweight construction including carbon fiber hoods and fenders plus a sport tuned suspension & aerodynamics package ensure the driving experience lives up to expectation for those looking for ultimate performance on or off the track

25 Lamborghini Huracan

Get ready for a revolutionary drive. The Lamborghini Huracan Performante is an outstanding piece of engineering, combining powerful performance and exquisite design to create the ultimate sports car experience. With its 5.2-liter V10 engine producing 640 horsepower and 442 lb-ft of torque, it's capable of reaching speeds over 200 mph in 2.5 seconds flat - making every journey thrilling yet safe with advanced aerodynamics utilizing both lightweight materials such as carbon fiber bodies and active systems for unparalleled stability at high velocities.

26 Alfa Romeo 4C

The Alfa Romeo 4C is a thrilling combination of power and agility. With its turbocharged 1.75-liter four-cylinder engine producing 237 horsepower, paired with an ultra responsive six speed dual clutch transmission and carbon fiber monocoque chassis that boasts a formidable power to weight ratio, this compact sports car means business - zooming from 0 to 60mph in just 4.1 seconds before hitting speeds up to 160 mph! A true driver's delight both inside the cabin and out, there's no better way for thrill seekers looking for their perfect match on four wheels than this sleek Italian supercar icon.

27 Datsun 280Z

The iconic Datsun 280Z was a legendary sports car of the '70s that provided an unforgettable driving experience. Making its debut in 1975 and produced up until 1978, it featured sharp handling along with power from a 2.8-liter inline six-cylinder engine producing 170 horsepower and 177 lb-ft of torque - propelling the vehicle to 120 mph top speed combined with 0 to 60 acceleration times at 8.5 seconds! A perfect blend between classic style and performance engineering made this model one for history books.

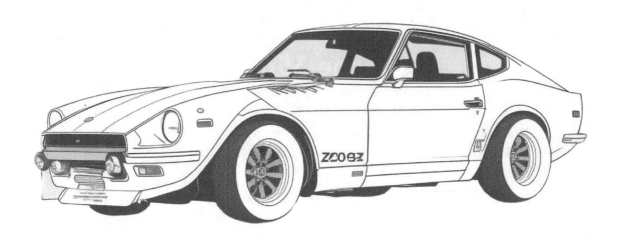

28 Porsche 356

Porsche AG's iconic Porsche 356 has been admired by sports car fans since its debut in 1948. A classic performance machine, this luxurious two-door coupe or convertible boasts a top speed of 110 mph and 0-60 acceleration time of 12 seconds - powered by an air-cooled flat four engine offering 40 to 95 horsepower depending on the model! With sleek styling, superior handling characteristics and lofty build standards that have made it stand out from other models for over seven decades, there is little wonder why the Porsche 356 remains one of history's most beloved luxury sports cars.

29 Renault Clio RS

The Renault Clio RS 4 injects a thrilling dose of adrenaline into everyday driving. The sleek, aggressive design hints at the power lurking beneath its hood - 1.6-liters of turbocharged fury that churn out 200 horsepower and 177 lb-ft of torque! With performance features like Brembo brakes and limited slip differential for improved grip on corners; as well as advanced technology such as touchscreen infotainment system with integrated navigation, it'll get you from A to B in style — all while maxing out at an impressive 143 mph top speed. Rise up your daily commute with this sporty pocket rocket today.

30 Honda S2000

Get ready to feel the power of Honda's ultimate two-seater sports car: the S2000. This vehicle packs a punch with its 2.0-liter engine and 237 horses under the hood, zipping from 0 - 60 miles per hour in an impressive six seconds flat! With sleek double wishbone suspension, limited slip differential for cornering thrills, lightweight frame, and 50:50 weight distribution meant for responsive performance--the S2000 serves up plenty of excitement on every journey you take it out on at speeds reaching up to 150 mph.

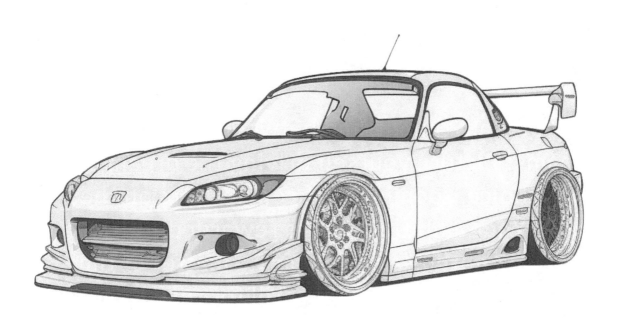

RACING DREAMS

Don't let anything stand between you and your dreams! Picture yourself driving the dream car of your choice, zooming past competitors on the track. Your ambition will be rewarded - with hard work and enthusiasm, it's only a matter of time until you experience that thrill for real. Keep pushing yourself every day to get closer to fulfilling your racing aspirations.

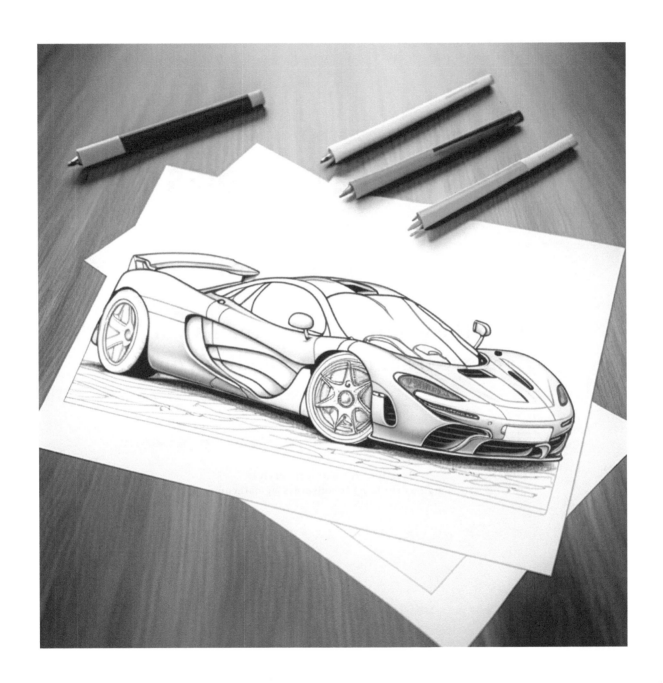

WANT FREE GOODIES ?

Email us at
racingdreamspress@gmail.com

Title the email "racing dreams vol1" and we'll send some goodies your way !

Questions & Customer service:
Email us at racingdreamspress@gmail.com

Made in United States
Cleveland, OH
03 December 2024